CUSTOM CONFECTIONS

YOURSELF

DELICIOUS DESSERTS
YOU CAN CREATE
and Enjoy!

by Jen Besel

CAPSTONE YOUNG READERS
a capstone imprint

Table of Contents

MOUTHWATERING DESSERTS

... Made by You!

Get ready! You're about to start making showstopping treats that look as good as they taste. In the mood to do some baking? Need a quick no-bake treat? Or do you just want to spruce up some store-bought goodies? You've come to the right place.

You don't need to be a professional baker to make custom desserts. With a few ingredients and some simple steps, you can create your own delicious treats. And you won't have to spend days in the kitchen to do it. But you can let your guests think you did.

So jump right in. What custom confection will you start with?

Convert It

The recipes in this book use U. S. measurements.
If you need metric measurements, here's a
handy conversion guide.

United States	Metric
¼ teaspoon	1.2 mL
½ teaspoon	2.5 mL
1 teaspoon	5 mL
1 tablespoon	15 mL
¼ cup	60 mL
⅓ cup	80 mL
½ cup	120 mL
⅔ cup	160 mL
¾ cup	175 mL
1 cup	240 mL
1 quart	1 liter
1 ounce	30 grams
2 ounces	55 grams
4 ounces	110 grams
½ pound	225 grams
1 pound	455 grams

Fahrenheit	Celsius
200°	90°
300°	140°
325°	160°
350°	180°
375°	190°
400°	200°
425°	220°
450°	230°

TOOLS

You'll need some kitchen tools to create mouthwatering treats. But don't worry. You probably have most of these in your kitchen already.

cookie cutters {1}

cake stands or serving platters {2}

fine sieve {3}

cake boards {4}

cutting board {5}

electric mixer {6}

springform pan and other cake pans {7}

edible glitter {8}

small melon baller {9}

rolling pin {10}

bowls {11}

spoons {12}

muffin tins {13}

cupcake liners {14}

lemon zester {15}

cooling rack {16}

candy thermometer {17}

small basting brush {18}

fondant smoother {19}

piping bags and tips {20}

angel food pan {21}

wax paper {22}

pastry cutter {23}

vinyl shape stencils {24}

tweezers {25}

pastry scraper {26}

fondant rolling pin {27}

baking sheets {28}

measuring spoons {29}

offset spatula {30}

CHECKERBOARD Cake

Roses are a sweet way to decorate any cake. But don't let the beauty stop there. Bake a cake with a gorgeous checkerboard of color that's sure to surprise and delight.

1 box white cake mix

1 box chocolate cake mix

food coloring

vanilla buttercream frosting, colored as you wish *(See page 110 for the recipe.)*

1 Mix the box of white cake mix according to package directions. Divide the batter into two bowls.

2 Mix up the box of chocolate cake mix according to package directions. Pour half the batter into another bowl, and save it for another use.

3 Add food coloring to one bowl of white batter. Stir until the color is blended.

4 Cover the insides of three round baking pans with nonstick cooking spray. Pour each bowl of batter into a greased pan. Bake the cakes according to package directions.

5 Allow the cakes to cool to room temperature.

6 Wrap each cake in two layers of plastic wrap. Put them in the refrigerator for at least one hour.

7 Remove the cakes from the refrigerator and unwrap them.

8 Center a plastic lid from an oatmeal container (or a round object of similar size) on one of the cakes. Cut around the lid. Then carefully remove the center piece of cake.

continued on next page

9 Repeat step 8 with the other two cakes.

10 Lay one of the outside rings of cake on a serving plate or cake board. Spread a thin layer of frosting around the inside ring. Then put an inside circle of a different color cake in the hole.

11 Spread a layer of frosting over the cake layer you made in step 10. Then lay another outside cake ring on top of the first. Frost inside the ring and fill with a different color center circle.

12 Repeat step 11 with the last two pieces of cake.

13 Spread a thin layer of buttercream frosting over the entire cake.

14 Fill a piping bag with frosting. Pipe large roses all around the side of the cake. Then do the same on the top. (For piping tips, go to page 110.)

15 Fill in the empty areas between the roses with a swoop of frosting that goes the same direction as the rose next to it.

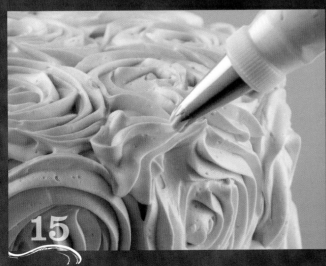

BLUEBERRY CHEESECAKE Tarts

Make these mouthwatering bites for your next party. The sugar cookie crust, blueberry filling, and cheesecake are a winning combination.

1 Preheat the oven to 325°. Spray a muffin tin with nonstick cooking spray.

2 Roll each precut piece of sugar cookie dough into a ball. Place one ball in each muffin cup.

3 Bake the dough for six to seven minutes or until golden brown. Remove from the oven. Press down the middle of each cookie to form a cup.

4 Beat the cream cheese, condensed milk, egg, and vanilla in a medium bowl until combined.

5 Drop 1 teaspoon of pie filling into each cup. Then pour 2 teaspoons of cream cheese mixture on top to fill each cup.

6 Bake the tarts at 325° for five minutes or until the cheesecake mixture is set.

7 When they're finished baking, carefully pop each tart out of the tin with a spoon. Set the tarts on a cooling rack.

8 When cool, top each tart with blueberry filling or fresh blueberries.

1 package refrigerated precut
sugar cookie dough

1 8-ounce package cream cheese, softened

¾ cup sweetened condensed milk

1 egg

1 teaspoon vanilla extract

blueberry pie filling

fresh blueberries, if desired

13

1 teaspoon cream of tartar

1 teaspoon salt

1 teaspoon baking soda

5 cups flour

1 cup granulated sugar

1 cup powdered sugar

1 cup butter, softened

2 eggs

1 cup vegetable oil

1 tablespoon vanilla extract

1 teaspoon almond extract

food coloring

edge royal icing (*See page 109 for recipe.*)

sprinkles and mini candies

HIDDEN PRESENT
Cookies

These fun cookies are as sweet inside
as they are outside.

1. Gather a large gift-shaped cookie cutter and a small square cutter. Then find a plastic container that's as tall as the gift cutter. Cover the inside of the container with plastic wrap. Set the container and cookie cutters aside.

2. Stir together the cream of tartar, salt, baking soda, and flour in a large bowl.

3. In another bowl cream together the sugars and butter. Beat in the eggs, then the oil.

4. Slowly beat the flour mixture into the sugar mixture. Finally, mix in the vanilla and almond extracts.

5. Split the dough into six balls. Knead food coloring into each ball. Then split each colored ball in half.

6. Press one half-ball into the bottom of the plastic-wrapped container.

7. Press a half-ball of another color into the container on top of the first. Continue layering the dough, alternating colors as you go, until you've put all the dough into the container.

8. Cover the dough with plastic wrap. Then put the container in the freezer for at least four hours.

continued on next page

9 Preheat the oven to 350°. Take the dough out of the freezer, and lift it out of the container by pulling up on the plastic wrap. Remove the plastic wrap from the dough.

10 Cut the dough into ¼-inch slices.

11 Line a baking sheet with parchment paper. Lay the dough slices on the sheet in rows of three. Bake for 12 minutes.

12 After taking the cookies out of the oven, press the gift-shaped cookie cutter into each slice. But don't lift the shape out just yet.

13 While the cookies are still hot, also use the square cookie cutter to press out the center area of one cookie in each row. Remove the center area and set aside.

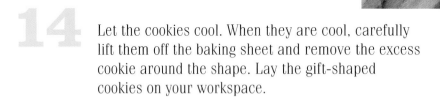

14 Let the cookies cool. When they are cool, carefully lift them off the baking sheet and remove the excess cookie around the shape. Lay the gift-shaped cookies on your workspace.

15 Put the royal icing in a piping bag. Outline one whole cookie with icing.

16 Lay a cookie with the center cut out on top of the icing. Fill the hole with sprinkles or candies.

17 Outline the filled cookie with icing, and lay another whole cookie on top.

}

18 Repeat steps 15–17 to finish the rest of the cookies.

19 Pipe royal icing onto the cookies to create bows. Let the icing harden for 30 minutes.

BLACK AND WHITE
Angel Food

Chocolate and orange are a surprising combination. But use the flavors in this layered angel food cake for a heavenly dessert.

1 box angel food cake mix

2 tablespoons + ¾ teaspoon unsweetened dark cocoa powder

1 teaspoon orange extract, divided

1 tablespoon + ¼ teaspoon orange zest

1¼ cups powdered sugar

3 tablespoons milk

1 orange

1. Preheat the oven to 350°.

2. Prepare the cake batter as directed on the package. Pour half the batter into another bowl.

3. Add 2 tablespoons cocoa powder to one bowl of batter. Gently fold the cocoa in.

4. Add ½ teaspoon orange extract and 1 tablespoon orange zest to the other bowl of batter. Gently stir.

Custom Tip

If you're not a fan of oranges, that's OK. Just leave out the orange extract and zest. Then garnish with your favorite fruit.

5. Pour the chocolate batter into an ungreased angel food cake pan. Pour the orange-flavored batter on top.

6. Bake the cake according to package directions. When the cake is finished baking, carefully remove the pan from the oven. Immediately turn the pan upside down and place it on top of an upside-down flower pot or glass. Let the cake cool completely in this position.

7. Once the cake is cool, set it upright. Loosen the cake from the sides of the pan by running a butter knife around the edges. Place a plate on top of the pan. Then flip the pan and plate together. The cake should sit on the plate when you remove the pan.

8. Pour the powdered sugar into a small bowl. Add the milk, and stir to create a syruplike glaze. Pour half of the glaze into another bowl.

9. Add ½ teaspoon orange extract and ¼ teaspoon orange zest to one bowl of glaze. Stir together. Drizzle the orange glaze over the cake.

10. Add ¾ teaspoon of cocoa to the second bowl of glaze and stir. Add a splash of milk if needed to get a syruplike consistency. Drizzle the chocolate glaze over the cake.

11. Cut the orange into thin slices and arrange on top.

RED VELVET
Cookies

Combine tasty red velvet cake with a sweet cream cheese filling, and you'll have treats that won't stay in the cookie jar for long.

1 box red velvet cake mix

2 eggs

1/3 cup oil

2 teaspoons vanilla extract, divided

4½ cups powdered sugar, divided

½ cup butter, softened

1 8-ounce package cream cheese, softened

1 Preheat the oven to 375°. Line two baking sheets with parchment paper.

2 Mix the cake mix, eggs, oil, and 1 teaspoon vanilla in a large bowl. The dough will be sticky.

3 Put ½ cup powdered sugar in a separate bowl.

4 Scoop out 1 heaping tablespoon of dough. Drop the dough into the powdered sugar. Completely cover the dough with sugar and roll into a ball. Then put the ball on a baking sheet. Repeat with the rest of the dough. Place each dough ball 3 inches away from other balls.

5 Bake the cookies for seven to 10 minutes. Let them set for two minutes in the pan before setting on a cooling rack.

6 Cream the butter, cream cheese, and 1 teaspoon vanilla in a large bowl. Slowly add 4 cups powdered sugar, mixing until the frosting is smooth.

7 Put the frosting in a piping bag.

8 Turn one cookie upside down. Pipe a generous amount of frosting on the cookie. Press another cookie on top. Repeat with all the cookies.

SWEETHEART
Cupcakes

Show how much you care with one sweet and surprising dessert. It's easier to do than you might think!

1 box white cake mix

1 box chocolate cake mix

cherry buttercream frosting
(See page 110 for recipe.)

½ cup semisweet chocolate chips

maraschino cherries

1 Spray an 8-inch square baking pan with nonstick spray. Make the white cake mix according to package directions. Pour 1½ cups of the batter into the greased pan. (Save the rest of the batter for some extra cupcakes or another small cake project.)

2 Bake at 350° for about 20 minutes or until a toothpick inserted into the center comes out clean. Let the cake cool completely.

3 Run a butter knife around the edges of the cake. Lay a cutting board on top of the pan. Carefully turn the board and pan over together. Lift the pan straight up, letting the cake sit on the cutting board. Then use a heart-shaped cookie cutter to press hearts out of the cake.

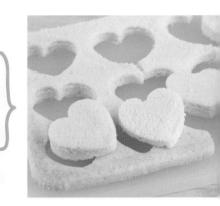

4 Put cupcake liners in a muffin tin.

5 Prepare the chocolate cake mix according to package directions. Pour 2 tablespoons of the chocolate batter into each liner.

6 Gently press a cake heart into the batter in each liner. The bottom of the heart should point down. Cover each heart with a bit more chocolate batter.

7 Bake the cupcakes at 350° for 24 to 26 minutes. When done, let the cupcakes sit in the pan for 10 minutes. Then transfer them to a cooling rack. Let them cool completely before frosting.

8 Fill a piping bag with cherry buttercream frosting. Pipe a generous amount of frosting on top of each cupcake.

9 Put the chocolate chips in a microwave-safe bowl. Melt the chips in the microwave on high for 30 seconds, stopping after 15 seconds to stir. Gently dry the cherries, then dip them into the melted chocolate. Finish each cupcake with a chocolate-covered cherry on top.

MINI APPLE Cakes

Celebrate autumn or the first day of school with these fun apple-shaped cake balls. They'll make raking leaves or cracking the books just a little bit sweeter.

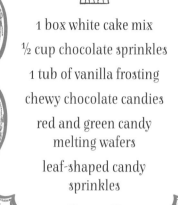

1 box white cake mix

½ cup chocolate sprinkles

1 tub of vanilla frosting

chewy chocolate candies

red and green candy melting wafers

leaf-shaped candy sprinkles

1 Preheat the oven to 350°. Spray a baking pan with nonstick cooking spray. Prepare the cake mix, and bake according to package directions.

2 Let the cake cool completely. Then crumble the cake into a bowl so there are no large pieces. Pour in the chocolate sprinkles.

3 Add frosting to the bowl of cake pieces one spoonful at a time. Mix well after each addition. Your mixture should be a moist dough that you can shape into balls. If it seems too dry and falls apart easily, add more frosting. You'll probably use almost a full tub of frosting.

4 Scoop out 1 tablespoon of cake mixture. Gently shape the mixture into an apple shape. Place the apple on a baking sheet lined with wax paper. Roll the rest of the mixture into little apples. Then refrigerate them overnight.

5 Cut the chewy chocolate candies into thin strips. Roll the strips into tubes to look like apple stems.

6 Melt the red and green candy wafers according to package directions.

7 Dip one end of a lollipop stick into one of the bowls of melted candy. Press the candy-coated end into the flat bottom of an apple. Place the apple back on the baking sheet to let the candy dry while you repeat with the rest.

8 Dip an apple into one color of melted candy. Tap the stick on the bowl to remove any excess candy. Before the candy coating dries, press in a chocolate stem and a leaf-shaped candy. Press the sticks into a foam block to let the apples dry.

9 Repeat step 8 with the rest of the apples. Once the candy coating is completely set, carefully pull the apples off the sticks, if you wish.

½ cup butter

4 ounces semisweet
baking chocolate

1 cup powdered sugar

2 whole eggs

2 egg yolks

6 tablespoons flour

4 pieces chewy caramel

sea salt

Molten Caramel Cake

Ooey, gooey salted caramel steals the show in this delicious take on a traditional lava cake.

1 Preheat the oven to 425°. Spray four custard cups or four cups in a muffin tin with nonstick cooking spray.

2 Put the butter and chocolate in a large microwave-safe bowl. Heat until the butter melts. Then stir until the mixture is smooth.

3 Add the powdered sugar to the chocolate mixture, and stir until smooth. Then stir in the eggs and egg yolks.

4 Pour the flour into the chocolate mixture and stir just until combined.

5 Divide the chocolate mixture among the cups.

6 Cut each caramel piece into four quarters. Press a generous pinch of sea salt into each caramel quarter.

7 Press four salted caramel quarters into the batter in each cup. Make sure the batter covers them.

8 Bake the cups for 12 to 13 minutes or until the sides are set but the center is soft.

9 Let the cakes rest for two minutes. Then turn the cakes out onto plates.

10 Sprinkle the top of each cake with sea salt. Serve right away.

Custom Tip

Here's an easy way to separate an egg. Hold your washed hand palm up over a bowl. Have someone crack an egg into your hand. Let the egg whites drip between your fingers. The yolk will be in your palm.

27

PERFECT
Pie Pops

Any food is more fun when it's on a stick!
Turn your favorite pie into a pie pop
that's perfect for any occasion.

2 boxes refrigerated pie
crusts, softened

canned pie filling, any flavor

1 egg, beaten

white sparkling sugar

1. Preheat the oven to 450°. Line two baking sheets with parchment paper.

2. Unroll two pie crusts onto a floured work surface. Use a round cookie cutter to punch out eight circles from each crust. Lay half of the circles on a baking sheet.

3. Press one craft stick or thin dowel into the center of each circle on the baking sheet.

4. Spoon 1 tablespoon pie filling onto each circle. Leave about ½ inch around the edge.

5. Use small shape cookie cutters to punch out shapes from the centers of the circles left on the work surface.

6. Brush the edges of the circles on the baking sheet with egg. Then lay one circle with a cutout shape over each circle on the baking sheet. Gently press the edges together. Then use a fork to make indents around the edges.

7. Repeat steps 2–3 with the other two full crusts.

8. Cut eight of the circles into ¼-inch wide strips.

9. Spoon 1 tablespoon pie filling onto each circle. Then brush the edges of these with egg.

10. Lay three strips over the filling on each circle. Then weave three more strips over and under the first strips. Press the edges together on each pie pop.

11. Brush the tops of all the pie pops with egg. Sprinkle with sparkling sugar.

12. Bake for 10 to 13 minutes or until golden. Let the pies rest on a cooling rack before eating.

29

PB AND J CHEESECAKE
Brownies

Turn basic brownies into
showstoppers with a cheesecake
topping swirled with everyone's favorite
combo—peanut butter and jelly.

1 Preheat the oven to 325°. Line a 9x13-inch baking pan with parchment paper, letting some hang over the sides.

2 Make the brownie mix according to package directions. Spread the batter in the pan.

1 box brownie mix

20 ounces cream cheese, softened

½ cup granulated sugar

1½ tablespoons flour

½ tablespoon vanilla extract

½ cup sour cream

2 eggs

1 cup creamy peanut butter

1 cup raspberry jam

3 Beat the cream cheese, sugar, flour, and vanilla until well blended. Add the sour cream. Then mix in the eggs, one at a time, just until blended.

4 Spread the cream cheese mixture over the brownie batter.

5 Put the peanut butter in a microwave-safe bowl. Melt for 15 to 30 seconds until the peanut butter is a bit runny.

6 Drop spoonfuls of jam and peanut butter on top of the cream cheese. Pull a knife through the cream cheese to swirl the jam and peanut butter.

7 Bake for 40 minutes or until the center is almost set.

8 Let the brownies cool completely in the pan. Once they're cool, lift the parchment paper straight up to remove the brownies from the pan. If desired, use cookie cutters to cut shapes out of the brownies. Or you can just cut them into basic squares.

BOSTON CREAM Bites

Make these tasty treats in two sizes—regular and mini. Then guests can choose just how much deliciousness they can handle.

1 Preheat the oven to 350°. Spray a regular-size muffin tin and a mini muffin tin with nonstick spray.

2 Make the cake mix according to package directions.

3 Fill the regular-size cups with ⅓ cup batter. Bake for 18 to 21 minutes or until a toothpick inserted in the center comes out clean.

4 Let the cupcakes sit in the pan for about 15 minutes. Then move them to a cooling rack.

5 Fill each mini cup with 2 tablespoons of batter. Bake at 350° for nine to 11 minutes or until a toothpick inserted in the center comes out clean.

6 Let the cupcakes sit in the pan for about 15 minutes. Then move them to a cooling rack.

7 When both the regular and mini cupcakes are completely cool, cut off the top of each cupcake. Carefully set the tops aside.

1 box yellow cake mix

2 cups cold milk

2 3.4-ounce packages instant vanilla pudding mix

3 cups whipped topping, thawed

2 cups dark chocolate chips

1½ cups heavy cream

~continued on next page~

8 Beat the milk and pudding together for two minutes. Then gently fold in the whipped topping.

9 Fill a piping bag with the pudding mixture. Pipe a generous amount of pudding mixture on top of each cupcake bottom.

10 Press the cupcake tops back on the cupcakes.

11 Pour the chocolate chips and cream into a small microwave-safe bowl. Heat uncovered for 30 to 60 seconds or until the chips are smooth when stirred.

12 Spoon melted chocolate over the top of each cupcake. Let the chocolate set for at least one hour.

STAINED GLASS Cookies

Brighten up plain old sugar cookies with a stained-glass look. Created with melted hard candies, this will be one kind of glass you won't mind breaking.

1 Preheat the oven to 350º. Roll out the cookie dough according to package directions. The dough should be about ¼ inch thick.

2 Use a large cookie cutter to cut out as many shapes from the dough as you can.

3 Use a smaller cookie cutter to punch out a shape inside each larger shape. Remove the small shapes and set aside.

4 Cover a baking sheet with parchment paper. Place the large shapes on the baking sheet.

5 Separate the hard candies by color. Put each color in a separate zip-top bag. Smash the candies into small pieces.

6 Fill the inside hole of each cookie with candy pieces. Fill the holes just up to the top edge. You can use one color or mix colors for a fun effect.

7 Bake the cookies for six to eight minutes or until the candy is melted. Let the cookies cool completely on the pan before removing them.

8 Color the edge royal icing as you wish. Then put it in a piping bag. Pipe icing around the outer edges of the cookies. Let the icing dry for at least one hour.

1 package refrigerator sugar cookie dough

colorful hard candies, unwrapped

food coloring

edge royal icing *(See page 109 for recipe.)*

LAYERED FRUIT *Pastry*

Pile on the sweetness with this delicious and beautiful dessert. Traditionally called a mille-feuille (pronounced mil-FWEE), this delicate confection is sure to please.

2 cups whole milk

6 tablespoons granulated sugar

3 tablespoons cornstarch

½ teaspoon banana extract

fresh strawberries, washed and patted dry

puff pastry from your local bakery

fresh blueberries, washed and patted dry

1 Mix the milk, sugar, and cornstarch in a large pan. Stir until the sugar is almost dissolved.

2 Put the pan on the stove over medium heat. Bring the mixture to a boil, stirring constantly.

3 Continue stirring as the mixture simmers for three to five minutes. When the mixture becomes very thick, remove the pan from the heat.

4 Stir in the banana extract.

5 Pour the pastry cream mixture into a bowl and cover with plastic wrap. Refrigerate the mixture while you work on steps 6 and 7.

6 Cut the strawberries into thin slices.

7 Cut three thin slices off the puff pastry.

8 Fill a piping bag with pastry cream. Pipe cream onto one of the puff pastry slices.

9 Arrange a layer of strawberry slices on the cream. Then lay another pastry slice on top of the strawberries.

10 Pipe cream on the second pastry slice. Arrange blueberries on top of this layer. Then top with the last slice of pastry.

11 Pipe cream on the top layer. Then arrange strawberries and blueberries on top for a pretty finish.

39

A TRIO OF *Truffles*

With three varieties of these tasty truffles, there's sure to be something for everyone.

Cake Batter Truffles

1 Beat the butter and sugar together. Blend in the vanilla. Add the cake mix and flour, and mix completely.

2 Beat in milk, 1 tablespoon at a time, until you have a dough consistency.

3 If desired, mix sprinkles into the dough.

4 Roll the dough into one-inch balls. Place the balls on a parchment-lined baking sheet. Refrigerate for 15 minutes.

¼ cup unsalted butter, softened

¼ cup granulated sugar

½ teaspoon vanilla extract

½ cup yellow cake mix

¾ cup flour

3-4 tablespoons milk

2 tablespoons sprinkles, if desired

Cookie Dough Truffles

1 Beat the butter and sugars together. Add the flour and vanilla, and mix completely.

2 Beat in milk, 1 tablespoon at a time, until you have a dough consistency.

3 Pour in the mini chocolate chips. Mix the chips into the dough.

4 Roll the dough into 1-inch balls. Place the balls on a parchment-lined baking sheet. Refrigerate for 15 minutes.

¼ cup unsalted butter, softened

¼ cup granulated sugar

½ cup brown sugar

¾ cup flour

½ teaspoon vanilla extract

3-4 tablespoons milk

½ cup mini chocolate chips

~continued on next page~

Dark Chocolate Truffles

1 Melt the dark chocolate according to package directions. Let cool.

2 Beat the cream cheese and sugar in a large bowl until smooth. Then stir in the melted chocolate and the vanilla.

3 Put the mixture into the refrigerator for at least one hour.

4 Roll the dough into 1-inch balls. Place the balls on a parchment-lined baking sheet. Refrigerate for 15 minutes.

6 ounces dark baking chocolate

4 ounces cream cheese, softened

1½ cups powdered sugar

¾ teaspoon vanilla extract

Decorating Truffles

1 Take the truffles out of the refrigerator and allow them to come to room temperature.

2 Melt the candy wafers according to package directions.

3 Gently drop one truffle into the candy melt. Carefully press the truffle into the candy with a fork to cover the top. Slide the fork under the truffle and slowly lift it out of the candy. Slide the fork over the lip of the bowl to scrape off any excess candy. Then gently place the covered truffle back on the baking sheet.

4 If desired, cover the truffle with nuts or sprinkles while the candy is still wet. Repeat the process with the other truffles.

5 Let the truffles set for at least 30 minutes.

6 If you wish, melt a second color of candy wafers. Drizzle the candy over the truffles. Let set for another 30 minutes.

candy melting wafers

chopped almonds or walnuts

sprinkles

STUFFED
Strawberries

Take strawberries from sweet to spectacular with this recipe. Pipe in a tangy cheesecake filling for an easy but elegant treat to eat.

fresh strawberries, washed and patted dry

1 8-ounce package of cream cheese, softened

½ cup powdered sugar

1 teaspoon vanilla extract

2 ounces dark chocolate, chopped into small pieces, if desired

1 Cut the stems off all the strawberries.

2 Cut the tips off the strawberries so they can stand upright. Place the strawberries on a baking sheet.

3 Scoop out the center of each strawberry, leaving a hole for filling.

4 Beat the cream cheese, sugar, and vanilla until fluffy.

5 Put the cream cheese mixture into a piping bag.

6 Fill each strawberry with cream cheese mixture.

7 If you want a chocolate drizzle, put the chocolate in a microwave-safe bowl. Melt the chocolate in the microwave, stopping every 15 seconds to stir.

8 Once the chocolate is melted, drizzle it over the strawberries.

4 cups water, divided

2 boxes blue gelatin

1 box yellow gelatin

1 cup sweetened condensed milk, divided

2 envelopes unflavored gelatin

8 gelatin snack cups, any flavors

GELATIN *Art*

Turn gelatin into a work of art. The layering takes a little time, but the results will be well worth the wait.

1. Spray an 8-inch square baking pan with nonstick spray. Bring 3½ cups of water to a boil in a saucepan.

2. Empty one package of blue gelatin into a bowl. Pour in 1 cup of boiling water. Stir until the gelatin is dissolved. Pour the hot liquid gelatin into the baking pan. Put the pan in the refrigerator for 20 minutes.

3. While the blue gelatin is cooling, pour ¼ cup of the yellow gelatin into a bowl. Add ¼ cup of boiling water to the bowl, and stir until the gelatin is dissolved. Then add ¼ cup of condensed milk and mix to combine. Pour this mixture into the pan over the blue layer. Refrigerate for another 20 minutes.

4. Pour ½ cup cold water into a bowl and sprinkle the unflavored gelatin on top. Let it sit for two minutes.

5. Pour 1 cup of boiling water into the unflavored gelatin. Stir until the gelatin is dissolved. Add ½ cup of condensed milk and stir. Let this mixture sit until it reaches room temperature.

6. Run a knife around the edges of the premade gelatin cups to pop the gelatin out. Cut the gelatin into cubes. Then sprinkle the cubes on top of the yellow layer in the pan. }

7. Pour the white gelatin you made in step 5 over the cubes in the pan. Refrigerate for another 30 minutes. }

8. Repeat step 3 to create a yellow layer on top of the cubes. Then repeat step 2 to create a blue layer on top. Once it's done, cut the gelatin art into squares or other shapes before serving.

FROSTY FROZEN
Cakesicles

These frozen cheesecake treats will be a hit with kids of all ages.

Mint Chocolate Cakesicles

1 Crush the sandwich cookies. Put ½ cup of the crumbs into a large bowl. Pour the remaining crumbs into another bowl and set aside.

2 Combine the cream cheese, yogurt, sugar, milk, peppermint extract, and a few drops of green food coloring in the bowl with the ½ cup of crumbs. Mix until well combined.

3 Pour the cream cheese mixture into ice pop molds, leaving 1 inch at the top. }

4 Mix the reserved cookie crumbs and butter together. Press 1 tablespoon of the cookie mixture into each mold. }

5 Press a craft stick into the center of each mold. Put the molds in the freezer for at least six hours.

36 chocolate sandwich cookies, divided

1 8-ounce package cream cheese, softened

¼ cup plain Greek yogurt

¾ cup powdered sugar

⅓ cup milk

¼ teaspoon peppermint extract

green food coloring

2 tablespoons melted butter

~continued on next page~ 49

Strawberry Cakesicles

1 Blend the cream cheese, yogurt, sugar, milk, and strawberries until well combined.

2 Pour the cream cheese mixture into ice pop molds, leaving 1 inch at the top.

3 Mix the graham cracker crumbs and butter together in a small bowl. Press 1 tablespoon of graham cracker mixture into each mold.

4 Press a craft stick into the center of each mold. Then put the molds in the freezer for at least six hours.

1 8-ounce package cream cheese, softened

¼ cup plain Greek yogurt

¾ cup powdered sugar

⅓ cup milk

¾ cup frozen strawberries

½ cup graham cracker crumbs

2 tablespoons melted butter

Change It Up

You can make frozen cheesecake pops in all kinds of flavors. Try these other variations.

Switch the frozen strawberries for another kind of frozen fruit. Blackberries, raspberries, or blueberries are great options.

Dip the frozen pops in melted chocolate to make a candy shell.

Follow the strawberry cakesicle recipe, but replace the plain yogurt with peach yogurt and add diced peaches.

Divide the cream cheese, yogurt, sugar, and milk into three bowls after mixing. Add a different frozen fruit to each bowl. Blend the contents of one bowl. Then fill each mold one-third full. Repeat with the other two bowls, layering the different fruit flavors in the molds, and then freeze. You'll end up with layered cakesicles with three fruit flavors.

Edible Flowers

Don't use flowers from your backyard for any desserts. They could have poisonous pesticides on them. Go to a flower shop, and ask the florist for pesticide-free edible flowers.

1 cup granulated sugar

½ cup corn syrup

½ cup water

food coloring

candy flavoring oil, any flavor

small edible flowers, such as violets, lavender, violas, or marigolds

EDIBLE FLOWER Lollipops

These treats are both gorgeous and tasty. They make great gifts too. Simply wrap them in colorful cellophane and tie with a ribbon. Give someone's day a "pop" of sweetness.

1 Spray a lollipop mold with nonstick cooking spray.

2 Mix the sugar, corn syrup, and water in a saucepan. Clip a candy thermometer to the side of the pan. Bring the mixture to a boil without stirring.

3 When the mixture reaches 250°, add food coloring until you get the desired color.

4 Continue to cook the mixture, without stirring, until it reaches 300°. Then take the pan off the stove.

5 Stir in two or three drops of flavoring oil.

6 Quickly pour the mixture into the shapes of the mold. Place a flower or two on each shape. Use lollipop sticks to gently press the flowers down into the hot candy. Then press the sticks into the candy, using the stick holes in the mold. You'll need to work fast because the mixture will harden quickly.

7 Let the lollipops sit for about 15 minutes.

8 Pop the lollipops out of the mold.

53

EDIBLE CUPS OF
Mousse

White chocolate mousse is delicious on its own. But put the mousse in candy cups, and you have a dessert that's hard to beat.

1 bag candy melting wafers, any color

2 4-ounce packages white chocolate instant pudding mix

2½ cups milk

1 16-ounce tub whipped topping, thawed

1 Place the melting wafers in a small zip-top bag. Leave the bag open and microwave on the defrost setting for 30 seconds. Squeeze the melted candy to one corner. If the wafers are not soft yet, microwave on defrost for 30 seconds more. Snip off the corner of the bag.

2 Place a mini muffin liner in each cup of a muffin tin.

3 Pipe about 2 teaspoons of melted candy into the bottom of one liner. Use a small paintbrush to coat the sides of the liner with melted candy. Make sure all parts of the liner are coated.

4 Repeat step 3 until you've done all the liners in the pan. Then put the pan with candy-coated liners in the freezer for at least one hour.

~continued on next page~

5 Pour the pudding mixes into a large bowl. Add the milk. Stir until the ingredients are well mixed.

6 Gently fold the whipped topping into the pudding. Chill this mousse mixture in the refrigerator for at least 1 hour.

7 Take the cups out of the freezer. Gently peel away the paper liners.

8 Fill a piping bag with the mousse mixture. Pipe mousse into each candy cup.

9 If you wish, top each cup with toasted hazelnut pieces.

Toasting Hazelnuts

Toasted hazelnuts will make this treat extra special. Making them does require a little baking. But the process is so easy, and the result is so good.

3 cups water

4 tablespoons baking soda

1 cup hazelnuts

1 Bring 3 cups of water to a boil in a saucepan. Then carefully add the baking soda and nuts. The mixture may bubble, so be careful.

2 Let the nuts boil for three minutes. Then pour them into a colander and rinse well with cold water. Use your fingers to slip the skins off the nuts.

3 Lay the peeled nuts on paper towels and pat dry.

4 Preheat the oven to 350°. Spread the nuts evenly on a baking sheet. Bake them for 15 minutes, stirring every five minutes.

5 When they're done baking, pour the hot nuts into a bowl and allow them to cool. Then chop the cool nuts.

ROLLED WAFER COOKIE *Cake*

Turn a simple cream cheese and pudding dessert into an edible masterpiece. Lovely and tasty, rolled wafer cookies add a special touch and a delicious crunch.

1 Cut the cookies into 2½-inch pieces and set aside. Put the leftover 1-inch pieces in a zip-top bag and crush them.

2 Spray a springform pan with nonstick cooking spray. In a small bowl, combine the cookie crumbs, graham cracker crumbs, and butter. Then press the mixture onto the bottom of the pan.

3 In a large bowl, beat the cream cheese and sugar until smooth.

4 Add the pudding mixes and milk to the cream cheese mixture. Beat until mixed.

5 Fold the whipped cream into the pudding mixture.

6 Spoon the cream cheese mixture over the crust. Cover the pan with plastic wrap and refrigerate for at least six hours.

7 Just before serving, remove the sides of the pan. Arrange the 2½-inch cookie pieces around the dessert and press gently into the sides.

8 Garnish the cake with chocolate curls.

1 can rolled wafer cookies

½ cup graham cracker crumbs

¼ cup melted butter

1 8-ounce package cream cheese, softened

1 cup granulated sugar

2 3-ounce packages instant pudding mix, any flavor

3 cups whole milk

1 cup whipped cream

chocolate curls *(See page 111 for recipe.)*

LOVELY LAYERED
Parfaits

Whether you're craving chocolate or need a fruity treat, these cups of layered goodness will be just what you're looking for.

Chocolate Parfaits

1 Turn a glass or small jar upside down. Press the glass into the chocolate cake to cut out circles.

2 Make the pudding according to package directions.

3 Drop two large spoonfuls of whipped cream into each glass. Then press a cake circle into each glass on top of the cream.

4 Sprinkle in some toffee pieces. Pour chocolate syrup on top. Then drop two more large spoonfuls of pudding into each glass.

5 Repeat steps 3 and 4 until you've filled the glasses.

1 8-inch square chocolate cake

butterscotch instant pudding mix

whipped cream

toffee pieces

chocolate syrup

Raspberry Parfaits

1 Cut the pound cake in half horizontally so you have two thin cakes. Turn one parfait glass or small jar upside down. Press the glass into the pound cake to cut out circles.

2 Whisk the jam and water together in a small bowl.

3 Drop two large spoonfuls of whipped cream into each glass. Then press a cake circle into each glass.

4 Drop two large spoonfuls of jam on top of the cake pieces. Add three or four raspberries on top of the jam.

5 Repeat steps 3 and 4 until you've filled the glasses.

1 10-ounce frozen pound cake, thawed

8 tablespoons raspberry jam

2½ tablespoons water

whipped cream

fresh raspberries

STRIPED ICE CREAM *Cake*

With ice cream, pound cake, and jam, this dessert is layered with tasty flavors. Even better, you won't have to heat up the kitchen making it.

1 loaf frozen yellow pound cake, slightly thawed

1 loaf frozen chocolate pound cake, slightly thawed

½ cup strawberry jam, divided

2 pints vanilla ice cream, divided

1 pint raspberry sorbet

1 Line a 9x13-inch baking pan with plastic wrap.

2 Cut both loaves of pound cake into 1-inch slices. Arrange the yellow slices in the pan so they cover the bottom. Set the chocolate slices aside.

3 Spread ¼ cup of jam on the pound cake layer. Then spread one pint of vanilla ice cream over the jam. Put the pan in the freezer for 30 minutes.

4 Spread a pint of sorbet over the ice cream layer. Freeze for another 30 minutes.

5 Spread the last pint of ice cream over the sorbet layer.

6 Spread the remaining jam on the chocolate pound cake slices. Put the cake slices on the ice cream layer, jam side down.

7 Cover the pan with plastic wrap. Then place the pan back in the freezer for at least eight hours.

8 Once the cake is frozen, turn the pan over on top of a cutting board, and let the cake slide out. Remove the plastic wrap. Cut off the edges to make them neat. Then cut the cake into slices.

Custom Tip

Beat the sorbet and ice cream with an electric mixer to make them easier to spread.

FROZEN LEMONADE
Poppers

You won't be able to eat just one of these tangy frozen treats—and neither will your guests!

1 Crush the graham crackers into fine crumbs.

2 Stir the cracker crumbs, butter, and sugar together in a small bowl.

3 Spray a mini muffin tin with nonstick cooking spray.

4 Spoon 1 heaping teaspoon of the cracker mixture into each muffin cup.

5 Press the cracker crumbs down firmly to cover the bottom of each cup. A small glass can help with this part. Then put the muffin tin in the refrigerator while you work on the filling.

6 In a large bowl, fold together the whipped topping and condensed milk. Gently stir in the lemonade concentrate.

7 Spoon 1 tablespoon of the whipped topping mixture into each muffin cup. Then cover the tin with plastic wrap, and put it in the freezer for at least eight hours.

8 When you're ready to eat, run a knife around the edge of each treat to pop it out.

9 Top each bite with a blackberry.

---

4 sheets graham crackers

2 tablespoons melted butter

1 tablespoon granulated sugar

8 ounces whipped topping, thawed

1½ cups sweetened condensed milk

¾ cup frozen lemonade concentrate, thawed

fresh blackberries, washed and patted dry

¾ cup whipped cream

8 ounces mascarpone cheese, softened

3 cups brewed coffee, cooled

about 30 ladyfingers

cocoa powder

TASTEFUL *Tiramisu*

Tiramisu is an elegant, delicious dessert. Its creamy layers are a beautiful way to end a meal.

1 Line a loaf pan with plastic wrap, letting the plastic hang over on all sides.

2 Gently mix the whipped cream and mascarpone cheese together.

3 Pour the coffee into a bowl.

4 Dip an entire ladyfinger into the coffee. Then lay it in the loaf pan. Repeat with six more ladyfingers, arranging them on the bottom of the pan.

5 Spread one-third of the whipped cream mixture over the cookies.

6 Sprinkle cocoa powder over the whipped cream mixture.

7 Repeat steps 4–6 two more times to create a total of three layers.

8 Cover the pan with plastic wrap and refrigerate overnight. When you're ready to serve, lift the tiramisu out of the pan using the plastic wrap. Remove all the plastic wrap before slicing.

CHOCOLATE ALMOND
Dessert Bars

Combine almond flavor and chocolate for a treat that's perfect for a picnic or a party. Put it all on a pretzel crust, and you have a dessert that won't last long.

2½ cups crushed pretzels

½ cup granulated sugar

1½ cups melted butter, divided

½ teaspoon almond extract

3 cups powdered sugar

3 tablespoons milk

½ cup butter

2 cups milk chocolate chips

candy melting wafers

whole almonds without shells

1 Mix the crushed pretzels, sugar, and 1 cup melted butter together in medium bowl.

2 Spray a 9x13-inch baking pan with nonstick cooking spray. Then firmly press the pretzel mixture onto the pan bottom.

3 Beat ½ cup melted butter, almond extract, powdered sugar, and milk together.

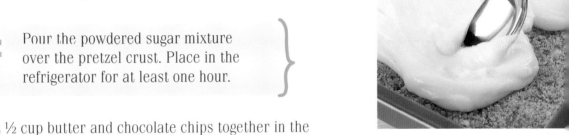

4 Pour the powdered sugar mixture over the pretzel crust. Place in the refrigerator for at least one hour.

5 Heat ½ cup butter and chocolate chips together in the microwave, stirring every 20 seconds until melted.

6 Melt ½ cup candy wafers according to package directions.

7 Spread the chocolate over the powdered sugar layer in the pan. Drop small spoonfuls of the melted candy on top of the chocolate. Pull a butter knife through the melted candy and chocolate to create swirls.

8 Before the topping sets, quickly press almonds into the bars. Space them evenly so you can cut the dessert into pieces later. If you wish, melt a few more candy wafers, and drizzle the candy over the almonds.

9 Refrigerate the bars for at least 30 minutes.

OOEY, GOOEY
Turtle Cake

Bring the magic of turtle candies to the table with this terrific spin on terrific flavors.

1 Pour 2 cups of chocolate chips into a large bowl.

2 Pour ½ cup of cream into a small saucepan. Heat the cream over low heat just until the cream is hot and bubbly on the sides.

2½ cup semisweet chocolate chips, divided

1 cup heavy cream, divided

11 ounces melting caramels

2 teaspoons sea salt

2½ cups pecan halves

3 Pour the hot cream over the chocolate. Stir until the chocolate is melted and the mixture is smooth. Let the chocolate cool for two hours.

4 Spray a springform pan with nonstick cooking spray.

5 Whip the cooled chocolate mixture for about one minute. Then pour it into the pan.

6 Put the caramels, salt, and ½ cup heavy cream into a microwave-safe bowl.

7 Microwave the caramels until melted, stopping to stir every 30 seconds.

8 Pour the caramel mixture into the pan over the chocolate layer. Sprinkle the pecans and ½ cup chocolate chips on top of the caramel layer.

9 Let the cake rest at room temperature for at least four hours. Before serving, remove the pan's outside ring. Transfer the cake to a serving plate.

PAINTED Cookies

Add a splash of color to store-bought cookies with homemade gel. Put a little edible glitter in the gel, and your dessert will really sparkle.

1 Mix the water and cornstarch together in a small microwavable bowl.

2 Stir in the corn syrup and vanilla.

3 Microwave the mixture on high for one minute, 30 seconds or until the mixture boils and turns clear.

4 Set the bowl on your work surface to cool. Whisk the mixture every couple of minutes.

½ cup cold water

2 tablespoons cornstarch

½ cup corn syrup

1 teaspoon clear vanilla

gel food coloring

edible glitter

light-colored cookies with smooth tops, such as lemon wafer cookies

5 When the mixture is at room temperature, mix in food coloring to create the color you want. Add 1 or 2 teaspoons of edible glitter to the mixture.

6 Pour the colored gel into a small squeeze bottle. Squeeze the gel onto the cookies in any shape or design you want. You could even write names or initials on the cookies.

7 When you're done, put the cookies on wax paper to set for at least one hour.

CREAM PUFF *Tree*

Let dessert be the centerpiece of your next
gathering. Everyone will crowd around the table
for this deliciously beautiful display.

about 100 frozen cream
puffs, thawed

caramel syrup

chocolate syrup

¼ cup white chocolate
chips

red gumdrops

1 Carefully wrap an 8-inch foam cone with aluminum foil. Then place the cone on a serving plate.

2 Cover three baking sheets with wax paper. Divide the cream puffs into three groups and put them on the baking sheets.

3 Drizzle caramel syrup over the cream puffs on one baking sheet. Then drizzle chocolate syrup over the cream puffs on another baking sheet.

4 Put the white chocolate chips in a microwave-safe bowl. Heat for 30 seconds on the defrost setting. Stir. Heat again until the chips are melted and smooth when you stir them. Drizzle the melted white chocolate over the puffs on the third baking sheet.

5 Let the puffs sit in the refrigerator for about 30 minutes.

6 Stick a toothpick into one cream puff. Then attach the cream puff to the foam cone. Continue adding cream puffs around the bottom of the cone, alternating the chocolate, caramel, and white chocolate ones. Put the puffs as close together as you can.

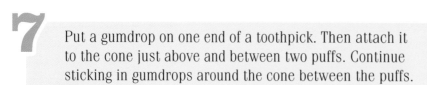

7 Put a gumdrop on one end of a toothpick. Then attach it to the cone just above and between two puffs. Continue sticking in gumdrops around the cone between the puffs.

8 Continue placing cream puffs and gumdrops around the cone. The puffs should stack directly on top of each other. The gumdrops should fill the spaces between the puffs. Top off the tree with a trio of puffs.

vanilla buttercream
frosting *(See page 110
for recipe.)*

food coloring

chocolate buttercream
frosting

5 cupcakes, any flavor

sprinkles

mini chocolate chips

1 sugar cone

maraschino cherry

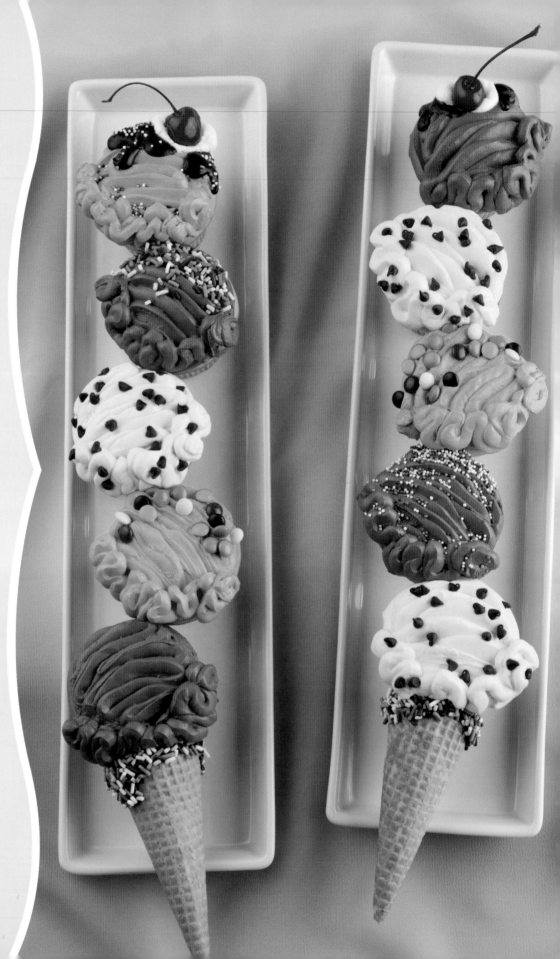

ICE CREAM CONE
Cupcakes

Have everyone screaming for ice cream with this fun spin on cupcakes.

1. Divide the vanilla buttercream frosting into bowls.

2. Add food coloring to all but one of the bowls and stir well. Leave one bowl white.

3. Put each color of frosting, including the chocolate, into a separate zip-top bag and close tightly. For each bag, press the frosting down into one corner, and snip off the tip of the bag.

4. Pipe one color of frosting onto a cupcake with a swirling motion. After the top of the cupcake is covered, add extra swirls of frosting to one edge to make the cupcake look like a scoop of ice cream.

5. Garnish the frosted cupcake with sprinkles, chocolate chips, or whatever candies you like.

6. Repeat steps 4 and 5 with the rest of the cupcakes, using the colors of frosting as you wish.

7. Arrange the cupcakes on a serving platter so they look like they are sitting on top of each other.

8. Spread chocolate frosting around the top edge of the cone. Then press sprinkles into the frosting.

9. Lay the cone under the bottom cupcake. Gently press the cone into the cupcake so it looks as if the cupcake is in the cone.

10. Finish the arrangement with a cherry on top.

TIERED FONDANT Cake

Build up layers of deliciousness with this classic tiered cake. Using a sweet marshmallow fondant, you can make your cake and eat it too.

2 10-inch square cakes, any flavor

vanilla buttercream frosting
(See page 110 for recipe.)

2 6-inch square cakes, any flavor

powdered sugar

uncolored marshmallow fondant
(See page 108 for recipe.)

1 Trace a 6-inch square cake board on a piece of scratch paper, and cut it out. Set the paper square aside.

2 Put one 10-inch cake on a 10-inch square cake board. Spread a layer of vanilla buttercream frosting on the top. Lay the second 10-inch cake on top.

3 Repeat step 2 with the 6-inch cakes and a 6-inch cake board.

4 Frost the tops and sides of the layered 10-inch cake with vanilla buttercream.

5 Generously dust your work surface with powdered sugar. Roll the fondant out into a large square. It doesn't have to be perfect. You just want to make sure you have it large enough to cover your cake.

6 Lay the rolling pin along the bottom edge of your fondant square. Curl the edge of the fondant around the pin, and roll the fondant onto it.

7 Unroll the fondant over the 10-inch cake.

~continued on next page~

8 Gently smooth the fondant on the top of the cake using a circular motion. You can use a fondant smoother or your hands.

9 Smooth the sides of the cake.

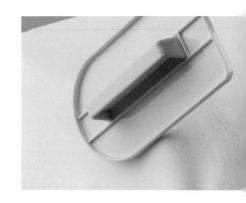

10 Cut off any extra fondant at the bottom of the cake.

11 Repeat steps 4–10 with the layered 6-inch cake.

12 Center the paper square on top of the 10-inch cake. Gently trace around the paper with a toothpick. Remove the paper square.

13 Gently push a cake dowel all the way into the cake at one corner of the traced square. Mark the height of the cake on the dowel with a pencil. Remove the dowel and cut at the line. Cut four more dowel pieces the same height.

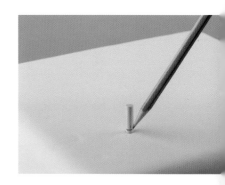

14 Press four dowels into the cake at the four corners of the traced square. Press one into the center.

15 Carefully place the 6-inch cake and cake board on top of the 10-inch cake along the dowel lines.

16 Wrap ribbon around the bottom of the 6-inch cake, covering the cake board. Attach the ribbon to the cake with a dab of vanilla buttercream.

17 Repeat step 16 on the bottom cake.

18 If you wish, arrange pesticide-free flowers on the cake tiers. Attach each flower with a dab of buttercream.

2 tablespoons water

2 tablespoons powdered egg white

fresh edible flowers, such as violets or impatiens, with stems removed *(See note on page 52 about edible flowers.)*

¼ cup granulated sugar

flood royal icing *(See page 109 for recipe.)*

food coloring, if desired

cupcakes, any flavor

SUGARED FLOWER
Cupcakes

Go from plain cupcake to stunning confection
with just a little icing and a flower on top.

1. Cover a baking sheet with wax paper and set aside.

2. Combine the water and powdered egg white in a small bowl. Beat together with a fork.

3. Use a small paintbrush to cover a flower with egg white mixture.

4. Hold the flower over an empty bowl. Sprinkle sugar over the flower. Lay the flower on a baking sheet.

5. Repeat steps 3–4 with the other flowers. Let the flowers dry overnight.

6. If desired, add a few drops of food coloring to the royal icing and stir. Then pour the icing into a piping bag or small squeeze bottle.

7. Pipe icing over the top of one cupcake, starting in the center and moving out in a circular motion. Gently shake the cupcake to spread the icing into a smooth layer.

8. Arrange sugared flowers on top of the icing while it's still wet.

9. Repeat steps 7 and 8 with all the cupcakes. Let the icing dry for at least one hour.

SIMPLY STENCILED Cake

Take cake from drab to fab with just a stencil and frosting. Go wild and crazy or fun and frilly. It's all up to you!

Cake Stencils

Any clean vinyl stencils can be used to decorate a cake. Look for stencils in your local hobby supply store. You'll want small designs for the sides and a large design for the top.

2 9-inch round cakes, any flavor

vanilla buttercream frosting (*See page 110 for recipe.*)

food coloring

marshmallow fondant, colored as you wish (*See page 108 for recipe.*)

powdered sugar

sugar pearls

1 Level the cakes by cutting off the rounded dome on each one. Set one cake on a cake board. Spread buttercream frosting on top of the cake. Then set the second cake on top of the first.

2 Spread a thin layer of frosting over the sides and top of the stacked cake.

3 Generously sprinkle powdered sugar over your work surface. Use a rolling pin to press the fondant into an 18-inch circle. Roll the fondant onto the pin, and then gently lay it over the stacked cake.

4 Smooth any wrinkles in the fondant. Then trim away excess at the bottom.

5 Color the buttercream frosting as you wish.

6 Carefully hold a small vinyl stencil against the side of the cake. Have a partner help you hold it in place. Carefully spread buttercream over the stencil. When you've filled in all the spaces, carefully pull the stencil straight off the cake.

7 Wipe off the stencil, then reposition it on the side of the cake, aligning it with where you left off. Spread frosting over the stencil again. Continue all around the cake.

8 Place a large stencil on top of the cake. Spread buttercream as you did on the sides. Lift the stencil straight up when you're done.

9 Carefully place sugar pearls in the buttercream.

ROYALLY ICED Cookies

Ever wonder how they get those gorgeous designs on cookies? Well, the secret is out! With royal icing, toothpicks, and a little practice, you'll be decorating your own eye-catching cookies in no time.

edge and flood royal icing
(See page 109 for recipe.)

food coloring

sugar cookies

1. Divide the edge royal icing into bowls. Color each bowl of icing as desired. Divide and color the flood icing just as you did with edge icing. Pour each icing into a separate piping bag.

2. To create hearts, pipe edge royal icing around the outside edge of a cookie. Then fill in the shape with flood icing of the same color. While the icing is still wet, pipe small dots of flood icing of a different color on the cookie. Drag a toothpick through the center of each dot to make a heart.

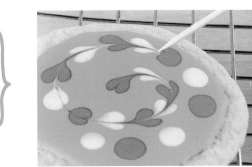

3. To create chevrons, pipe edge royal icing around the outside edge of a cookie. Then fill in the shape with flood royal icing of the same color. While the icing is still wet, pipe straight lines of other colors of flood icing across the cookie. Starting at the top of the cookie, drag a toothpick through the lines. Repeat as many times as you wish, always starting at the top.

4. To create starbursts, pipe edge royal icing around the outside edge of the cookie. Then fill in the shape with flood royal icing of the same color. While the icing is still wet, pipe circles on the cookie, one inside the next. Starting in the center of the cookie, drag a toothpick in a straight line through the circles. Go back to the center and repeat in different spots around the cookie.

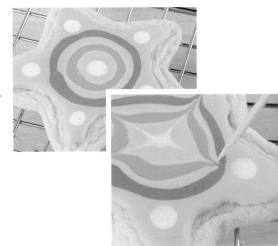

4 9x13-inch cakes,
any flavor

food coloring

vanilla buttercream frosting
(See page 110 for recipe.)

marshmallow fondant,
colored as you wish
(See page 108 for recipe.)

PILE-OF-BOOKS *Cake*

Love a good book and a good dessert? Bring these two loves together with this pile-of-books cake. These are the kinds of books you can really sink your teeth into.

1. Cut a piece of cardboard so it's 9x11 inches. Cut two 8x10-inch pieces. Then cut one piece that's 4½x6½ inches. Cover each cardboard piece with aluminum foil. These will be your cake boards.

2. Level the top of each cake. Also trim off any crusty edges so you have four neat rectangular cakes.

3. Cut 2 inches off a short side of one cake to make a 9x11-inch cake.

4. Cut 3 inches off a short side of another cake. Then trim off 1 inch from one long side. Then cut the cake in half horizontally, so you end up with two thin 8x10-inch cakes.

5. Cut a third cake in half so you have two 4½x6½-inch cakes.

6. Place the fourth 9x13-inch cake on a large wooden cutting board or large serving plate.

7. Color some buttercream as you wish. Spread the frosting over the top and one long edge of the cake.

8. Spread white frosting on the other three sides of the cake. While the frosting is still wet, drag the tines of a fork gently through the white frosting to make it look like pages.

continued on next page

9 Gently drag a thin spatula or the handle of a wooden spoon through the frosting along the colored long edge. This should look like where the book's cover would bend.

10 Place the 9x11-inch cake and the two 8x10-inch cakes on the cake boards of the same sizes. Then repeat steps 7–9 with each cake.

11 Put one of the 4½x6½-inch cakes on the same size cake board. Spread buttercream frosting on top. Then set the second cake on top. Frost this thick cake as you've done the others. You should now have five separate books.

12 Press dowels into the 9x13-inch cake where the corners of the 9x11-inch cake will sit. Also press one into the middle. Trim the dowels so they don't stand taller than the top of the cake.

13 Gently stack the 9x11-inch cake on top of the first cake over the dowels.

14 Repeat steps 12–13 to stack the rest of the cakes. Then pipe frosting along the bottom edges of each book to make it look as if there's a bottom cover.

15 Generously dust your work surface with powdered sugar. Roll out the fondant. Use alphabet-shaped cutters to punch out letters to add titles to the books. Also cut out decorations, such as diamonds for the spines, if you wish.

16 Let the letters and decorations dry for about one hour. Pipe a bit of buttercream onto the back of each fondant letter or decoration, and stick them onto the cake.

FARM FRIENDS
Cake Pops

Turn cake balls into adorable farmyard animals. Your friends will squeal with delight.

1. Crumble the cake into a bowl so there are no large pieces.

2. Add a spoonful of frosting to the crumbled cake. Mix well. Continue adding spoonfuls of frosting and mixing until the mixture is a moist dough that you can mold into balls. You'll probably use most of a tub of frosting.

3. Cover a baking sheet with wax paper. Roll the cake dough into 2-inch balls. Arrange on the baking sheet.

4. Melt a small amount of white melting wafers according to package directions.

5. Dip one end of a lollipop stick into the melted candy. Then press the coated stick end into a cake ball. Repeat with all the balls.

6. Place the cake balls with sticks into the freezer for about 20 minutes. Then let them come to room temperature before moving to the next step.

7. To make a cow, dip a cake ball into melted white candy. Place a red mini candy-coated candy on as a nose. Use two mini chocolate chips for horns. Press the lollipop stick into a block of foam, and let the candy dry for at least 30 minutes. Use a small paintbrush to apply melted chocolate wafers as spots. Use a black edible-ink pen to draw eyes and nostrils. Let the candy dry again.

8. To make a pig, cut a pink round candy in half. Dip a cake pop in melted pink candy wafers. Put the candy halves on as ears. Use a full pink round candy for a nose. Let dry. Then use a black edible-ink pen to draw on eyes, mouth, and nostrils.

9. To make a chick, dip a cake pop in melted yellow candy wafers. Press orange candy hearts into the ball to look like a beak. Press on flower pastels for feet. Also press in small white candy hearts along the top of the cake pop. Let dry. Use a black edible-ink pen to draw eyes.

1 9x13-inch cake or
2 9-inch round cakes,
any flavor

1 tub of frosting, any flavor

white, pink, chocolate,
and yellow candy
melting wafers

red mini
candy-coated candies

mini chocolate chips

black edible-ink pen

pink round candies

orange and white
candy hearts

orange flower-shaped
pastels

EDIBLE Decorations

Prepare to be amazed with this surprising dessert decoration. With just gelatin, water, and a paintbrush, you can create edible bows and butterflies to top any creation.

To Make the Gelatin

1 Put the water into a small microwaveable bowl. Stir in food coloring to your desired color.

2 Add gelatin to the water. Stir until there are no clumps.

3 Microwave the mixture for 20 seconds. Then let the mixture sit for about 10 minutes.

4 Use a spoon to scrape away the layer of foam that settles on top of the gelatin.

5 Reheat the bowl of gelatin for about 10 seconds or just until it's a warm liquid. It's now ready to use to create decorations.

6 tablespoons water

gel food coloring

1 tablespoon unflavored gelatin

edible glitter, optional

continued on next page

Making Gelatin Shapes

1 Use a paintbrush to brush the warm liquid gelatin into the cavities of a gelatin mold. Make sure you cover the entire surface, but don't leave liquid puddling inside.

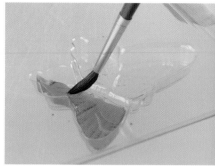

2 If desired, sprinkle the wet gelatin with edible glitter.

3 Let the gelatin set for about one hour.

4 Gently pop the gelatin shapes out of the mold. Trim away any excess gelatin, if necessary.

5 Press the gelatin shapes into freshly frosted cupcakes. Or pipe a bit of extra frosting onto a frosted cake and press the shapes into it.

Making Gelatin Bows

1 Use a paintbrush to paint the entire surface of a flexible chopping mat with liquid gelatin. Go over the mat three or four times to get a good coverage. Set the leftover gelatin aside. Let the gelatin set for about one hour. As it hardens, the gelatin might curl up a bit.

2 Lift the dry gelatin paper off the mat. Cut it into 1-inch wide strips. Then cut each strip in half lengthwise.

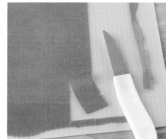

3 Reheat the bowl of gelatin for about 10 seconds or just until it's a warm liquid.

4 Paint one end of a gelatin strip with a bit of warm liquid gelatin. Fold the strip over to make a loop, pressing the ends together until they are stuck. Repeat with 15 more strips.

5 Arrange six loops in a circle with the ends pointing toward the middle. Glue the loops together by painting them with a bit of liquid gelatin and pressing until they stick. Use a long lollipop stick to help you pick up and press the loops.

6 Add more loops to the center of the circle, offsetting the loops as you build up the bow. Paint on liquid gelatin as glue to stick the loops to each other. You'll finish by adding a loop standing up in the middle.

7 Pipe a bit of frosting onto a frosted cake where you want the bow. Press the bow into the frosting.

DUNKED & DIPPED
Treats

This is one of the easiest and most entertaining desserts around. Dip and dunk all kinds of treats—from pretzels to strawberries. Get your friends together and have fun dunking your treats together.

1 Pour sprinkles and nuts into separate small bowls.

2 Melt the chocolate and white chocolate melting wafers according to package directions.

3 While the chocolates are still warm, dip a treat into one flavor of chocolate about half way.

4 Pour sprinkles or nuts over the treat, if you want.

5 If desired, drizzle the treat with the opposite color of melted chocolate.

6 Lay the treat on wax paper or stand it up in a jar. Let it rest until the chocolate has dried.

7 Mix and match chocolates and toppings on the other cookies, pretzels, and strawberries. You could even experiment with dipping different kinds of cookies or fruit.

sprinkles

chopped nuts

chocolate melting wafers

white chocolate melting wafers

pretzel rods

biscotti cookies

chocolate chip cookies

strawberries, washed and patted dry

BIG-EYED OWL Cake

Decorate your way to hoots of
happiness. A simple smeared dot
technique gives this bird its feathers.

1 10-inch round cake, any flavor

chocolate buttercream frosting
(See page 110 for recipe.)

2 6-inch round cakes, any flavor

food coloring

vanilla buttercream frosting

2 chocolate-covered cookies

2 red candy-coated candies

1 Put the 10-inch cake on your work surface. Lay a 6-inch round cake pan on the edge of the cake so it overlaps about 2 inches. Cut along the pan edge to remove an oval from the large cake. Then move the pan over and repeat the cut so you have two oval cutouts.

2 Lay the cake pan on the edge of the 10-inch cake directly below the oval cutouts, again overlapping about 2 inches. Cut out an arch shape from the cake.

3 Place the cut 10-inch cake on an 18-inch round cake board. Spread chocolate buttercream frosting along the two cut edges at the top of the cake. Nestle the 6-inch cakes into the cuts. It should look like a body with two large eyes.

4 Cut one of the oval pieces from step 1 in half widthwise. Spread chocolate frosting on the sides of the pieces. Place them just above the eyes. Then place the arch-shaped piece of cake you removed in step 2 above the eyes to finish the head.

5 Spread chocolate frosting over the owl's wings, between the eyes, and on the head. Leave the eyes and the center of the body unfrosted.

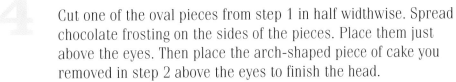

~continued on next page~ **101**

6 Color some vanilla buttercream orange. Put it in a piping bag with a round tip. Then fit another piping bag with a large round tip. Fill this bag with uncolored vanilla buttercream.

7 Pipe a row of round white frosting drops on the bottom of the body. Add a bead of orange frosting on top of each white drop. Use a spatula to flatten the frosting drops, then pull them up toward the eyes. Continue adding rows of frosting drops and pulling them up until the body is covered in frosting feathers.

8 Use orange buttercream to frost the eyes. Then add drops of more orange frosting around the edges of the eyes. Use a spatula to flatten the frosting drops and pull them toward the center.

9 Set a chocolate-covered cookie in the center of each eye. Pipe a small white dot on each cookie and top with a red candy-coated candy.

10 Color a small amount of vanilla buttercream yellow. Put it in a piping bag with a round tip.

11 Pipe a triangle of yellow frosting between the eyes as a beak. Then pipe feet on the cake edge between the wings.

MONSTER *Brownies*

Take brownies to the wild side with a drizzle of frosting and some creepy eyes. They're the perfect mix of sweet and scary.

a pan of brownies

vanilla buttercream frosting
(See page 110 for recipe.)

food coloring

gummy rings

mini chocolate chips

mini marshmallows

mini candy-coated candies

1 Cut the brownies into squares, and remove them from the pan.

2 Separate the buttercream frosting into bowls. Color each bowl of frosting a different "monster-ific" color. Put each color into a separate zip-top bag. Squeeze the frosting down to one corner, and cut off the tip.

3 Pipe long, stringy lines of frosting across one brownie. Start each line in the center and work toward the edge, letting the frosting hang over the sides.

4 Make eyes by putting two gummy rings on top of the frosted brownie. Press chocolate chips into the holes in the rings.

5 Pipe another color of frosting on another brownie using the same technique as in step 3.

6 Make different eyes by setting marshmallows in the frosting. Put a dab of frosting on each marshmallow. Then stick a mini candy-coated candy on each dab of frosting.

7 Continue frosting the brownies and making eyes. Give some of your monsters one eye, and give others three eyes.

HEDGEHOG *Cake*

Go for the unexpected with this wacky hedgehog cake. With slivered almonds for spines and a marshmallow treat head, this cake will be a delicious surprise.

2 6-inch round cakes, any flavor

vanilla buttercream frosting
(See page 110 for recipe.)

crispy rice marshmallow treats

chocolate buttercream frosting
(See page 110 for recipe.)

1 round vanilla wafer cookie

3 brown candy-coated candies

slivered almonds

1 Lay a round cake on your work surface. Spread vanilla buttercream on top. Lay the second cake on top of the first.

2 Cut two sides of the layered cake off so you have two straight edges and two rounded edges. Stand the cake up on one straight edge.

3 Sculpt marshmallow treats into a head with a pointed snout. The head should be as tall as the cake stack and fit nicely against the straight edge. You can heat the treats in the microwave for about 15 seconds to make them easier to mold.

4 Put the body and head on a serving platter. Spread vanilla buttercream frosting over the face and the body.

5 Spread a thin layer of chocolate frosting over the snout. Use a fork to draw lines on the face to look like fur.

6 Cut a vanilla wafer in half. Press the halves into the cake just behind the face to make ears. Then add candy-coated candies as eyes and a nose.

7 Dip a slivered almond about half way into chocolate frosting. Then press the chocolate-covered end into the cake body. Continue dipping and pressing the almonds in until the entire body is covered in almond spines.

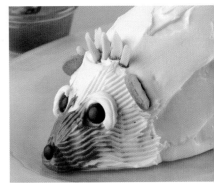

Marshmallow Fondant

4 cups plus some extra powdered sugar

8 ounces mini marshmallows

4 tablespoons water

food coloring, if desired

shortening

1. Generously dust your work surface with powdered sugar.

2. Put the marshmallows and water in a large microwave-safe bowl. Heat on high for one minute.

3. Stir the marshmallows until they are smooth.

4. If you want to color the fondant, add food coloring to the marshmallow mixture and stir.

5. Pour four cups of powdered sugar into the bowl. Stir until the mixture becomes too stiff to stir anymore.

6. Dump the sugar mixture onto your prepared work surface.

7. Coat your hands with shortening, then knead the sugar mixture. Continue kneading until the mixture becomes smooth. If the fondant starts sticking to your hands, put more shortening on them.

8. Once it's smooth, the fondant is ready to be rolled out and put on your cake.

Royal Icing

2 teaspoons meringue powder
2 tablespoons water
2 to 2½ cups powdered sugar

Edge and flood royal icings are made with the same ingredients. The only difference is how stiff you make the icing. Stiffer edge icing is perfect for creating outlines or decorations that need to hold a shape. Use flood icing to easily cover a large area.

Edge Icing

With an electric mixer on high, blend the ingredients together in a bowl for about four to five minutes. The icing is the right consistency when it forms little peaks that hold their shape. Pour the edge icing into a piping bag with a round tip to create designs or borders.

Flood Icing

Make a batch of edge icing. Then add water ½ teaspoon at a time, blending after each addition. The icing is ready when drips hold their shape for just a moment before they blend back into the icing. Spoon this icing onto a cookie or other dessert. Then use a toothpick or small paintbrush to spread it out.

Vanilla Buttercream Frosting

½ cup unsalted butter, softened
½ teaspoon vanilla extract
2 cups powdered sugar
1-2 tablespoons milk

1. In a large bowl, cream the butter and vanilla until fluffy.

2. Alternate adding sugar and milk until the ingredients are mixed well. The frosting should be thick, creamy, and spreadable. Scrape the sides of the bowl often with a spatula.

Variations

For chocolate frosting, follow the recipe above, and add ¼ cup unsweetened cocoa powder along with the sugar.

For peanut butter frosting, follow the recipe above but leave out the vanilla extract. Add in 1 cup creamy peanut butter and an extra tablespoon of milk.

For cherry frosting, replace the milk with maraschino cherry juice. Replace the vanilla with almond extract.

Piping Tips

To make a rose:

1. Put a 1mm open star tip on the piping bag. Hold the bag straight up from a cake top. Squeeze out a star.

2. Continue squeezing with even pressure, and swirl frosting around the star without lifting the bag up. When the top is covered, stop squeezing and pull the bag straight away from the cake.

To make a cupcake swirl:

1. Put a 1mm open star tip on the piping bag. Hold the bag straight up from a cake top. Squeeze out a star.

2. Continue squeezing with even pressure while lifting the bag slightly. Swirl frosting around the cake until the top is covered.

3. Continue squeezing as you move back to the center of the cupcake. Do another swirl on top of the first. Then stop squeezing and pull the bag straight away from the cupcake.

Chocolate Curls

3 ounces semisweet baking
chocolate

1 tablespoon shortening

1. Put the chocolate and shortening in a small microwavable bowl. Heat it for 20 seconds on high heat. Stir the mixture with a fork. If the chocolate isn't melted yet, heat it for another 20 seconds.

2. Place a baking sheet upside down on your work surface.

3. Pour the chocolate onto the center of the baking sheet.

4. Spread the chocolate out on the baking sheet to make a thin layer.

5. Put the chocolate-covered baking sheet in the freezer for two minutes.

6. Take the sheet out of the freezer. Scrape a metal spatula along the baking sheet, pushing the chocolate into curls.

7. Use toothpicks to lift the curls off the pan and place them on your dessert.

Custom Confections is published by Capstone Young Readers,
1710 Roe Crest Drive, North Mankato, Minnesota 56003
www.capstonepub.com

Library of Congress Cataloging-in-Publication Data
Besel, Jennifer M., author.
Custom confections: delicious desserts you can create and enjoy / by Jen Besel.
pages cm
Summary: "Step-by-step instructions teach readers how to create baked treats and no-bake desserts. Also includes
instructions for decorating cakes, cupcakes, cookies, and more"– Provided by publisher.
Audience: Ages 9-13.
Audience: Grades 4-6.
Includes bibliographical references and index.
ISBN 978-1-62370-136-9 (pbk.)
1. Desserts–Juvenile literature. 2. Cooking–Juvenile literature. I. Title.
TX773.B48657 2015
641.86–dc23   2014000245

Editorial Credits
Ashlee Suker, designer; Sarah Schuette, photo stylist; Marcy Morin, scheduler;
    Danielle Ceminsky, production specialist

Photo Credits
All images by Capstone Studio: Karon Dubke

Printed in the United States of America
in North Mankato, Minnesota..
072015   009124R